Paws for Reflection

50 DEVOS
— for —
DOG MOMS

LIVE YOUR FAITH

Paws for Reflection: 50 Devos for Dog Moms
Copyright © 2020 by DaySpring Cards, Inc.
First Edition, November 2020

Published by:

21154 Highway 16 East
Siloam Springs, AR 72761
dayspring.com

Written by: Janice Thompson
Cover Design by: Hannah Skelton

Printed in India
Prime: J2433
ISBN: 978-1-64454-812-7

Contents

Our Four-Legged Friends

...

Whether they're curled up at our feet or tearing up a roll of toilet paper when our backs are turned, dogs are a lovely addition to our lives. They have an uncanny sense of dedication and loyalty to us. Once bonded, they refuse to let go. They hang on like a hound with a ham bone.

If you've had the joy of knowing and loving a dog, then you already know what a blessing that precious companionship can be. They walk with us through the lowest valleys and bound ahead of us on life's many adventures, hoping we can keep up with them. With their cuddles, kisses, and wide, adoring eyes, they fill a void that humans couldn't possibly fill. They draw us closer to our Creator, the very One who placed that sense of faithfulness inside of them.

In the pages of this book you will find dog tails (er, tales) to remind you of God's abiding presence. May you be reminded that He's with you, no matter what you're going through.

Green with Envy

*Because the patriarchs were jealous of Joseph, they
sold him as a slave into Egypt. But God was with him.*

ACTS 7:9 NIV

• • •

Delilah, the little Yorki-Poo, was Mama's little baby.
She slept in the bed with Mama, rode in the car
with her to the park, and even shared nibbles of her
yummy people food.

Then, along came Roscoe, the Goldendoodle.
That giant oaf came lumbering into Delilah's life and
tried to flip things upside-down! Would you believe
he actually thought he could steal Mom's affections?

Wait! He was stealing her affections! Mom patted him on the head and called him "baby boy" and
scratched him behind his ears. What was up with that?

Delilah couldn't help herself. She snarled and
snapped at Roscoe whenever he came near Mom.
Surely he would learn his lesson eventually. He'd keep
his distance.

Turned out, the one who needed to learn the lesson was Delilah. It took some time for the jealous pup
to figure out that Roscoe was here to stay. She finally

curbed her envy and welcomed him as a friend.

Maybe you can relate. You've earned the favor of your boss. . .or your teacher. . .or a group of friends. You've been chosen time and time again to lead the Bible study group at church or sing the solo in the church choir. Now a "Roscoe" has come along and you're not the favored child anymore. You've had to move aside to make room for the new kid in town. . .and you're not having it.

It's time for a heart-check, sister! There's no room for jealousy with God's girls. Lay it down and let someone else have her turn. In fact, celebrate her moment with genuine heartfelt joy. You'll win a friend for life and become a little more like Jesus in the process.

No envy here, Lord!
I'm going to celebrate the victories of
the other women in my life.
Thank You for that reminder.

AMEN.

Guard Dogs

In a desert land He found him, in a barren and howling waste. He shielded him and cared for him; He guarded him as the apple of His eye.

DEUTERONOMY 32:10 NIV

• • •

It's a wonderful thing to have a dog that stands guard over his home. He's ready to take on any intruder who dares to enter. With his head cocked, ears tilted forward, and eyes wide open, your own personal canine alarm system sees and hears what his owners do not—the postal worker delivering mail, the car pulling up to the curb, the salesman approaching the door. He's keenly aware of all of the things that are invisible to you and stands ready to defend you at any cost.

In many ways your precious pooch is just mimicking the behavior of his Creator. He's paying attention so that he can protect the one he cares most about (you).

Here's a truth that should bring you great hope: There's no place you can go where the Lord doesn't see you. If you go to the depths (physically, spiritually, or psychologically) He's right there, hand extended. If you climb to the highest heights (Mt. Everest. . .or the top of your class in school) He's there, too. In the same way that Fido stands watch over his home, God is watching over you. Only, His reach is far greater than Fido's. He can handle foes with a single word (no barking necessary).

God's got you. He's got you when you're struggling. He's got you when you're soaring. He's got you when there are decisions to be made. He's got you when you feel you're on the wrong path. He's guarding you because you're the apple of His eye. You're His child, His beloved, His daughter. And because He loves you, He's going to fight for you with His life. In fact, He already did.

Lord, thank You for standing guard over me. You see every enemy that tries to come against me and You protect me at any cost. I'm so grateful.

AMEN.

3

A Shelter in the Time of Storm

You are a tower of refuge to the poor, O LORD,
a tower of refuge to the needy in distress. You are a
refuge from the storm and a shelter from the heat.
For the oppressive acts of ruthless people are like a
storm beating against a wall, or like the relentless
heat of the desert.

ISAIAH 25:4–5 NLT

• • •

Copper was the sweetest little dachshund on the planet, but he had one very troubling issue: He was a scaredy-cat. Er, scaredy-dog. Whenever a storm blew through, he would make a run for the bathroom and jump into the tub.

His owner, Annie, wasn't quite sure what to make of it. Many times, she would awaken in the night to the sound of barking coming from the bathroom. There she would find her precious pooch shivering and shaking in his porcelain hideaway. Turned out, he was great at getting in but couldn't get himself back out again.

Why the bathtub? A bit of research led her to the answer. Dogs feel grounded and safe in the tub during a storm. They leap over the edge to their porcelain safety net whenever they feel stressed or need an escape. Copper was doing what came naturally—protecting himself from the storm.

What about you? Where do you run when you need an escape from the storms of life? God wants to be your go-to hiding place. He longs for you to come to Him, not just when you're afraid, but whenever a storm of any kind hits. His name should be the first on your lips.

Are you walking through a storm right now? Call on the Lord. Jump into the safety of His arms. He will keep you grounded and safe, no matter how hard the winds might blow.

Lord, today I choose to run to You with my troubles. No more calling out to others first. You'll be my go-to from now on. Thank You for being my shelter in the time of storm.

AMEN.

4

Showing Up

Praise be to the God and Father of our Lord Jesus Christ,
the Father of compassion and the God of all comfort.

II CORINTHIANS 1:3 NIV

• • •

Lorena curled up in the bed, completely gutted by the news of her friend's death. She could hardly believe it. Just yesterday she'd laughed and talked with Rebecca. Now, suddenly. . .her friend was gone?

The tears came in earnest as Lorena tried to reason this out with God. A few moments into her grieving, a gentle nudge caught her attention. Her schnauzer, Buddy, pressed his nose against her arm until she turned to face him. She could barely see him through her tears.

The little darling crawled into her lap and rested his head on her shoulder. Then, as if to offer his own version of consolation, he licked her cheek. He seemed to know that she was hurting.

As the pup settled down in her lap, Lorena cuddled and cradled him, happy to have someone—something—to hold onto. In that moment, as she held him close, the peace of God wrapped itself around her. God used that little pup to bring undeniable comfort. Buddy didn't have to say a word. His presence was enough. It made all the difference in the moment and brought a sense of calm.

Perhaps you've been there. You've struggled through a crisis and the grief was unimaginable. Then, in a moment of undeniable holiness, God used your dog to minister to you—to bring cuddles, kisses, and comfort, just when you needed it. Or, perhaps He used a friend, someone who showed up with a casserole or a card saying, "I'm thinking of you."

Did you know that the Lord longs for you to minister to others in that same way—to be present in their affliction, to show up when they're hurting? Sometimes it doesn't take a word. . .just being there is enough.

Lord, my eyes are wide open. I don't want to overlook a friend in need. Teach me how and when to show up, Father, so that I can help those who are hurting.

AMEN.

5

Grumpy Gus

*Be devoted to one another in love.
Honor one another above yourselves.*

ROMANS 12:10 NIV

• • •

Hannah's little Min-Pin (miniature pinscher) was a Grumpy Gus. At nearly fourteen years old, he wouldn't put up with anything from anyone. If the other dog came near, he snapped. If someone moved him from his coveted spot on the sofa, he vocalized his discontent with a low growl at the back of his throat. If a visitor came in the home, he snarled and bared his teeth.

Talk about making his presence known! And the problems didn't end there. Gus had to be the first to eat, the first to receive Mom's affections, and the first to go out when the door opened (which was problematic since he moved at a much slower pace than the other dog). He definitely saw himself as the leader of the pack, a right gained with age.

Maybe you've known a few Grumpy Guses in your life. Maybe you are one. If you think about the people in your circle you'll have to conclude: Some people sour with age while others just get sweeter.

The sourpusses make things difficult for others while the sweethearts bend over backwards to share love and affection.

Which direction are you moving in? (Be honest!) As the years have come and gone, have you gotten kinder, sweeter, gentler to those around you? Or have you gotten more stubborn, more demanding, more inclined to prefer your own needs above those of others?

Don't be a Grumpy Gus. Age well. Make way for others. Don't insist on having your own way. Continue to act like Jesus. Be devoted to one another in love. (True love puts others first.) Make it a goal to honor one another (gasp!) above yourselves. It's not always easy, but the payoff is magnificent.

Lord, I want to age well. I want to look (and act) more like You with each passing day. Take any grumpy tendencies and remove them from me, I pray. Leave behind only the sweetness of Your Spirit.

AMEN.

6

Turn Your Heart toward Home

"Bring the fattened calf and kill it.
Let's have a feast and celebrate. For this son of mine
was dead and is alive again; he was lost and is found."
So they began to celebrate.

Luke 15:23–24 NIV

• • •

Luke enjoyed his position as lieutenant at the fire station. He knew the place inside and out. And though he had hosted several tours—everyone from children in school groups to senior citizens—he'd never invited a dog into the firehouse before.

Until Daisy. The haggard-looking coon hound wandered in off the streets, starving for both food and affection. Luke served up the scraps from the firefighters' most recent meal, which Daisy scarfed down. When Luke turned his back to tend to a hose that needed repair, the little prodigal slipped out of the station, into the night.

She returned the next afternoon and the afternoon after that. Before long, Daisy was a regular at the station, a mascot of sorts. Luke fell so in love with the dog that he decided to adopt her. Under his watchful eye she received the medical and emotional care that she needed, as well as great food. Before long, she was healthy, whole, and completely at ease. No more wandering for Daisy. She was home at last.

God shares a similar affection for His kids when they find their way back home. No matter where you've been, no matter what choices you've made in the past, you can come back to the Lord and He will care for you with the affection of the perfect Father that He is. He's got a feast prepared for you. There's always room at the table for one more. There you can be healed, and made completely whole. All wandering will cease.

So, what's keeping you? Come home to the Father today.

Lord, I'm so glad You welcome prodigals home again. You've got a place for all at Your table. I don't ever want to wander away from You, Father. Thank You for turning my heart toward home.

AMEN.

7

The Slippery Slope

For this reason, when I could stand it no longer, I sent to find out about your faith. I was afraid that in some way the tempter had tempted you and that our labors might have been in vain.

I THESSALONIANS 3:5 NIV

• • •

Jessup was a curious little pup, always getting into things. On those rare occasions when his owner, Margie, forgot to crate him when she went out, Jessup always managed to find something fascinating to do.

One summer afternoon he found a little more than he'd bargained for. There, on Margie's bedside table, sat a jar of something that looked slippery. Slimy. He used his nose to nudge the jar down to the floor, then made quick work of chewing it until the lid popped off.

Odd. The stuff didn't have much of a smell or taste, but as he licked it, Jessup noted that it went down with ease. Maybe too much ease. He continued to lick the slippery stuff until his tummy felt strange. Finally reaching the stopping point, he crawled under Margie's bed and slept. If only his stomach would stop gurgling.

Margie arrived home and called out to him but he didn't feel like seeing anyone. Not yet, anyway.

Only when she came looking for him did he offer a whimper.

"Jessup, why are you hiding under the bed?" She reached down, probably hoping he would come to her. Jessup crawled out, moaning all the while. "What's this?" Margie reached for the jar and then picked up the chewed lid. "Jessup! What in the world? Did you eat my petroleum jelly?"

So that's what they called the stuff. Ugh. It felt like jelly, all right. Jessup bolted toward the door, his stomach moving almost faster than his little legs.

Maybe you can relate to Jessup. You find yourself getting into messes that are hard to get out of. You have a difficult time saying no to temptation. Giving in rarely leads to a healthy life. Today, take the time to pray before sliding down that slippery slope!

Father, I don't want to give in! Give me the strength and the courage to say no when temptations come my way.

AMEN.

Caring for the Fledglings

Blessed are those who have regard for the weak;
the LORD delivers them in times of trouble.

PSALM 41:1 NIV

• • •

Elaine had a beautiful backyard—a spacious mani-cured deck and a lush, tropical garden where flowers of every sort bloomed in the springtime. She espe-cially loved filling her bird feeders. Watching the little sparrows come and go brought her hours of great joy.

Elaine's bird dog, Romeo, loved it too. On more than one occasion he raced to snatch the birds before they could fly away from the feeder. Thank good-ness they were faster than the rambunctious canine, though he loved the chase.

One spring morning Romeo carried a tiny fledg-ling into the house and dropped it on the floor. The poor little birdie could barely squeak out a sound. Elaine wrapped him in a dish towel and followed the dog back outdoors, where he led her to two more fledglings in the grass.

Her heart broke as she searched in vain for a nest in the tree above. Which of the many sparrows was the mama bird? Would she ever know? Elaine did her best to save those little birds, but in the end, none of them survived. Talk about heartbreaking!

Maybe you're like Elaine. You're in the business of helping/saving others. God loves your heart for the downtrodden! He cares about everyone, no matter their situation. And He's glad that you care too. He's in the "saving" business and some of that has spilled over to you.

Just make sure you're not trying so hard to save others that you forget to take care of yourself. And remember—enabling and caring are not the same thing. Pray for discernment to know the difference so that the fledglings can eventually learn to fly on their own, without your assistance.

I want to help them all, Father, but I know that only You can truly save. I'll do what I can and step back when You tell me to. Help me to know how much is enough, Lord.

AMEN.

I ONCE DECIDED NOT TO DATE A GUY BECAUSE HE WASN'T EXCITED TO MEET MY DOG. I MEAN, THIS WAS LIKE NOT WANTING TO MEET MY MOTHER.

Bonnie Schacter

A Good Reward

By grace you have been saved through faith. And this is not your own doing; it is the gift of God, not a result of works, so that no one may boast.

EPHESIANS 2:8–9 ESV

• • •

Dottie, the bull terrier, was a fast learner. She'd only been in her foster home for a matter of days when she figured out the sound of the treat jar. Foster mom Emily would rattle the lid of the jar and the other dogs would come running. They lined up at her feet, obedient pups, until they each received a yummy treat.

At first Dottie jumped up and down like a yo-yo, determined to be first in line. She tried to snatch the treat out of her foster mom's hand. She didn't understand this word "Sit!" Before long, however, she caught on. If you sat, Mom gave you a treat right away. And if you sat quickly, you even got a pat on the head and several words of affirmation. That felt good.

After a while, Dottie didn't even need to hear the treat jar in order to obey. She didn't depend on favors from Mom to offer the gift of obedience. The precious pup sat because she longed to please her owner. Mom's love was enough of a reward.

Maybe you can relate. You've tried to behave, to obey God's commands. You've done so out of a sense of obligation or in anticipation of something good from your heavenly Father. He does love to lavish His kids with sweet treats, after all. But you know what pleases His heart even more? When you obey simply out of your great love and respect for Him. What joy that brings to your Father's heart!

Today, challenge yourself to obey. . .just because. No arguing. No procrastinating. Just pure, holy obedience.

Lord, You don't need to load me up with treats to gain my obedience. I adore You! I'll do my best to obey, to follow Your lead in all things.

AMEN.

The Reflection in the Mirror

For now we see only a reflection as in a mirror;
then we shall see face to face. Now I know in part;
then I shall know fully, even as I am fully known.

I CORINTHIANS 13:12 NIV

• • •

Golden retriever Minnie caught a glimpse of her reflection in the hallway mirror. She stopped cold and turned to face what she thought was another dog—an intruder! How dare he enter her home without invitation! The yapping began in earnest. Minnie would protect her home and her master from this conniving canine, if it was the last thing she did.

Before long, the whole family was gathered around, laughing at Minnie as she barked with abandon at the other dog. Why did they find this so funny? Did they not realize she was trying to protect them from harm?

Then the strangest thing happened. Minnie noticed that whenever she turned her head, the dog in the mirror did the same. When she barked, it barked. When she jumped up and down, it followed suit. Was the crazy canine copying her, making fun of her, perhaps? It took some time to figure out the truth—she was staring at her own reflection.

Maybe you can relate to Minnie. You've stared at the reflection in the mirror and been confused by what you've seen. You've felt like yapping at the woman staring back at you. She bears some resemblance to the godly woman you want to be, but you wonder at times if she's mocking you.

God never called you to put your trust in your mirror image but, rather, in Him. Stop worrying so much about your reflection and let Him teach you who—and what—you're meant to be. You're created in His image and He's working hard to make sure you see that you're a beautiful reflection of Him.

Lord, I'll stop hyper-focusing on the woman in the mirror. She's flawed. . .but You are not. Thank You for creating me in Your image, Father.

AMEN.

Anticipating His Presence

The Lord is not slow in keeping His promise,
as some understand slowness. Instead He is patient
with you, not wanting anyone to perish, but everyone
to come to repentance.

II PETER 3:9 NIV

• • •

After a break-in in her neighborhood, Alyssa decided to have a security system installed in her house. It came with cameras so that she could keep an eye on things, even from work. More than once, her boxer, Brenden, triggered the alarm by running through the living room or jumping on the sofa. Whenever that happened, she would shut off the alarm, check the cameras, and laugh when she caught a glimpse of the pup playing with his favorite toy.

What intrigued Alyssa most about watching the dog through the cameras was his late afternoon routine. Every day around four-thirty Brendan would move into position by the front door. He sat, ears perched, waiting. And waiting. And waiting.

Brendan knew his master's habits and was ready

and waiting when Alyssa arrived home. He couldn't wait to greet her with his tail wagging and head nuzzled into her waistline.

Don't you love that picture of the dog's affection for his owner? Doesn't it warm your heart to know that canines anticipate spending time in their owner's presence? They're so anxious, in fact, that they will wait, no matter how long.

In the same way, your time with the Lord matters. He knows your habits, your customs, your schedule. He's right there, ears perched, waiting for you to join Him. And He longs for you to be just as ready, just as happy to hang out with Him.

> Lord, I'm so glad You want to be with me. My heart longs to spend time with You too. I'm so grateful You don't keep me waiting, Father. May I return that favor.
> AMEN.

Sit, Fido! Sit!

Sin will have no dominion over you,
since you are not under law but under grace.

ROMANS 6:14 ESV

• • •

"Sit, Fido! Sit!"

The first, and often easiest, command we humans give our canine companions is the instruction to "sit." When we finally get that feisty little pup's attention, when he actually sits and stares up at us with that "Now what?" expression on his face, we've crossed an invisible line in the sand. We've step into the role of master. He becomes our obedient child, working tirelessly to bring us joy. From there, we begin to ask other things of him—to stay, roll over, fetch, and so forth. We inch him forward in the obedience training.

Isn't that just how our relationship with Daddy-God should be? He has so much to teach us, but we're easily overwhelmed. We sign up for a Bible study, go to the first couple of classes, and then drop out. We set goals at the beginning of the year for our daily Bible and prayer time, then give up after only a couple of weeks. We don't learn to sit.

It's important to learn the most basic lessons because they are foundational for all of the lessons yet to come. The Lord has a lot to teach you, far more than you know now. But how will you ever learn if you can't get past the most basic commands?

Ask the Lord to show you if there's an area of your life where you need spiritual growth. If He responds with a yes, then sit quietly at His feet and allow Him to do that necessary work to grow your obedience.

Thank You for Your patience with me, Lord. Take me back to the basics so that I can "grow up" into the woman You've called me to be.

AMEN.

Annie, the Alpha Dog

He who is often reproved, yet stiffens his neck,
will suddenly be broken beyond healing.

PROVERBS 29:1 ESV

• • •

The little Chihuahua squared her shoulders, planted all four paws firmly on the ground, and glared at the family's new dog—a German shepherd mix—as if to say, "Hey, you. I'm the alpha dog here. You might win them over with your size, but I'm top dog in this family. Get used to it!" Despite her larger size, the shepherd eventually conformed to the house rules and Annie had her way. She taught that big dog a thing or two about who was boss and who was not.

Alpha dogs assert themselves, no matter what (or who) they're up against. They have to dominate and make the decisions for the group, even if their opinion isn't the popular one. Alphas must be the first to be served, the most likely to be coddled by the owner, and the favored child, even if it means nudging others out of the way to get what they want.

What about you? Do you have those same "alpha"

tendencies? Do you have to be right? Are you the decision maker in your group of friends? Are you always in charge? Do people look to you as top dog? Do you make it known that the buck stops with you and no one else? If so, it might be time to step aside for a change.

It's not easy to tuck your proverbial tail between your legs and let others take charge, especially when you're used to getting your own way. But make a concerted effort to allow your friends and acquaintances to shine. Back down, Annie! Give those other pups an opportunity to lead the way once in a while.

Lord, I don't want to be stubborn. I don't always have to be the alpha. Show me how to bend my will to Yours so that I'm more like You and so that others have an opportunity to shine once in a while too.

AMEN.

Chew on It

"Come now, let us think about this together," says the Lord. "Even though your sins are bright red, they will be as white as snow. Even though they are dark red, they will be like wool."

ISAIAH 1:18 NLV

• • •

If you've watched a dog chew on a bone, you know that nothing can distract him. He'll fight tooth and nail to defend his prize. If another dog—even a bigger one—comes along, he growls and bites down on the bone even harder, in anticipation of possibly losing it.

A dog can spend hours just gnawing on his precious bone (even a plastic one). And there are benefits to the canine as he chews. The bone sharpens and cleans his teeth. It also calms him down and keeps him still for a while (always a plus).

Maybe you've used the words "I just need to chew on that for a little while." If so, then you can surely appreciate that image of the dog with the bone. Some things in life just take time. They're not solved in a day. That's why it's so important to bring the issues you're facing to the Lord, to spend time in His presence. While you're together, you can reason things out with Him. You can chew on His Word and ask for ways to apply it to your life.

God wants you to hang on to your time with Him like a dog with a bone. Don't let go of it. Don't let anyone—or anything—snatch that bone. Hold tight to that precious time, no matter how hard the world tries to steal it away. There, in that quiet time, you will chew, chew, chew until you receive the answers you need to keep going.

Guard that bone, girl!

Lord, I've got some things to chew on. I need to spend time with You until some of these problems in my life are solved. I won't let anyone steal my time, Father. I'll hang onto it like a dog with a bone!

AMEN.

The Long, Low Shadow

Show me the wonders of Your great love, You who save by Your right hand those who take refuge in You from their foes. Keep me as the apple of Your eye; hide me in the shadow of Your wings.

PSALM 17:7–8 NIV

• • •

Dachshunds are sweet little things, but doxie owners will be quick to tell you that their little bundles of joy can be quite the handful. These feisty pups love to yap and don't always want anyone (or anything) taking attention away from them. They run on the stubborn side and are often difficult to train, but once you do get a handle on them, they're yours for life. They stick to you like glue and will dedicate their lives to loving you.

Some people call dachshunds "the long, low shadow." That's because they pick one person in the house to shadow constantly. You take a step, he takes a step. You sit down, he sits down. A dachshund simply has to be with his owner at all times. In fact, a doxie owner can barely get time alone in the bathroom. And talk about having a dog underfoot while cooking! That little darling is always right there, in need of constant reassurance that you're never going to leave her or forsake her.

Now think about your relationship with Jesus. He longs for you to shadow Him, to stick as close as that little doggie sticks to her owner. You're the apple of His eye, after all, and He loves to tuck you in at night under the shadow of His wings. It doesn't bother Him at all when you draw close. You're never underfoot or at risk of injury.

So, stick close! Don't go chasing other masters. Money, prestige, romance—none of these can give you what your heavenly Father can.

Lord, I will shadow You all of my days, pouring out all of my affection on You. There's no one like You, Father! I'll stick close because I know You'll take excellent care of me. I'm so grateful, Lord.

AMEN.

Belly Up

In all your ways submit to Him,
and He will make your paths straight.

PROVERBS 3:6 NIV

• • •

Goldie was a big girl—a full ninety pounds. As a pup, she always seemed to be in trouble. But what else was a purebred golden retriever to do? She was born to retrieve things, after all. She chewed up shoes, gnawed at the legs of her master's four-poster bed, and even mangled an expensive favorite purse.

Goldie's owner, Missy, was beside herself. If she couldn't get this ornery dog under control, she might have to consider re-homing her. And forget about correcting the naughty pooch! Every time she caught Goldie in the act, the sweet little thing just rolled over on her back and begged for a belly rub.

It took some time for Missy to realize that Goldie was offering her belly as an act of submission. But she did so as a ploy—to appease Missy in the moment.

We're a lot like that with God, aren't we? We deliberately disobey, then we're quick to act like we won't do it again. We offered rushed prayers: "God, I'm so sorry! I'll do better next time." But then we don't make an honest attempt to mend our ways when "next time" comes along.

It's time to go belly up, once and for all, girl! Submitting to the Lord means giving every area of your life to Him, not just today, but for the long haul. In all your ways submit to Him. That means even in your thought life. That cranky attitude? It has to go. Those gossip sessions with your bestie? Time to toss those to the curb. That snide comment you made to your hubby? Maybe you need to let that one go too.

Submission is the very best way to show the Lord that you mean business. What's holding you back? Today's the very best day to start.

Lord, I'm sorry for the many (many!) times I've said, "I'll change!" but then didn't. Today I do my best to submit to You in every area of my life. Thank You for Your patience, Father.

AMEN.

I FEEL SORRY FOR PEOPLE
WHO DON'T HAVE DOGS.
I HEAR THEY HAVE TO PICK
UP FOOD THEY DROP ON
THE FLOOR.

Anonymous

A Difference Maker

The Spirit you received does not make you slaves,
so that you live in fear again; rather, the Spirit you
received brought about your adoption to sonship.
And by Him we cry, "Abba, Father."

ROMANS 8:15 NIV

• • •

Georgianna loved to follow her local animal shelter's online posts. The faces of the dogs and cats always tugged at her heart. For years she watched the pictures go by in her newsfeed. Finally, she decided to do something to help. She gathered her grandchildren and they shopped for pet food, beds, dog shampoo, and several other items. When they dropped off the items at the shelter, Georgianna and her grandkids had a chance to see the dogs up close and personal.

The minute she laid eyes on the shivering little Chihuahua in a pen at the back of the room, Georgianna knew she had to do something. She filled out the paperwork and began the process of fostering.

Over a period of a year several dogs came and went from her home. She had a real opportunity to turn the lives of those little dogs around. She watched the skittish dachshund land in a furr-ever home with an elderly woman who needed cuddles. She helped a tiny mixed-breed pup overcome a terrible skin infection then go on to make a terrific family pet. Georgianna made a difference—one pet at a time.

Maybe you want to make a difference in your world but you feel inadequate. You think, "Who am I?" or "What gifts have I got to contribute that will make a difference?" Like Georgianna, you can make a difference, one life at a time. That friend at work who's down in the dumps? You can let her know she's loved. That child who's struggling in school? You can offer to tutor him. That elderly neighbor who's always alone? You can deliver home-baked cookies and engage her in conversation.

"Each one can reach one." Likely you've heard that expression before. It starts with a hand extended and a desire to make a difference.

Lord, I want to be a difference maker. There are people all around me who need TLC. Open my eyes that I might see the ones in need of an emotional lift, Father.

AMEN.

Tears for Natalie

My sacrifice, O God, is a broken spirit; a broken and
contrite heart You, God, will not despise.

PSALM 51:17 NIV

• • •

After a broken friendship Grace's heart grew hard.
She found herself holding people at arm's length. She
didn't want to let anyone in, for fear she would be
hurt again. So, she made up her mind to toughen up.

Then God sent a little beagle into her life. At first
Grace thought that Natalie was just like any other
puppy. After a few days, however, the little canine
began to display strange signs that were worrisome.
She couldn't seem to walk in a straight line and she
had seizure-like episodes. Grace took Natalie to the
vet and was told the pup had serious neurological
challenges as a result of an inoperable tumor on her
spine.

Determined she could save the little dog, Grace
cared for her around the clock. She changed her diet,
gave her supplements, did physical therapy—anything and everything to turn the situation around.

Over a period of months, Grace's hard heart began to soften—not just toward the dog, but toward the people around her, as well.

After a year and a half, Natalie's journey came to an end. Grace fell to pieces when the precious dog passed away. After some time, however, she realized the truth: God had used the little pup to open her heart once again. When the Lord offered an opportunity to repair her broken friendship, she took it. Grace and her friend were finally able to forgive each other and put their differences in the past.

Years passed, but many times Grace thought back to her journey with Natalie with great tenderness. Though the pup's time in Grace's care had been short, it had resulted in the most beautiful gift of all—a tender, forgiving heart.

Lord, I see how You've used my pup to soften my heart. I'm more affectionate, thanks to my dog-friends. Thank You for using them to shape me into the woman You've called me to be.

AMEN.

19

Picky, Picky!

Now eagerly desire the greater gifts. And yet I will show you the most excellent way.

I CORINTHIANS 12:31 NIV

• • •

Dogs can be picky eaters, just like humans. Take Buster, for example. The rat terrier turned his nose up at kibble, no matter how many different ways his owner offered it. He preferred wet food, thank you very much. And not just any wet food, but a particular brand. In a certain dish. At a certain time of day. Buster simply refused to eat until he got what he wanted.

His owner tried everything—kibble with broth, kibble with warm water to form a gravy. Nothing worked. The finicky pooch simply wouldn't eat it.

Humans can be finicky too. Whether we want to admit it or not, we often act a little, well, spoiled. We have a certain way we like things and it bugs us when someone else comes along and changes things up. We get our noses out of joint when friends or coworkers suggest an alternate plan or strategy. Let's face it: change is hard. . .and uncomfortable.

Oh, I know. . .you'd prefer to stay comfortable. Who wouldn't? But it's time to take a look at the many, many areas of your life where you refuse to budge and just ask yourself this tough question: do I need to make any adjustments?

Don't be so picky that you make things awkward or uncomfortable for those around you. Remember to put others first as often as you can and to do away with self-seeking motives. God desires you to be known as a woman of sacrifice, one who's as interested in those around her as she is in herself.

It's time to take inventory, precious girl. What attitudes can stay, and which need to go?

Lord, I want to live a sacrificial life, putting others' needs ahead of my own. I don't want people to see me as spoiled or picky. Show me how to bend my will to Yours, Father, and remove the desire to always have things my own way. Thank You in advance.

AMEN.

20

Lick that Problem!

O taste and see that the Lord is good.
How happy is the man who trusts in Him!

PSALM 34:8 NLV

• • •

Giant, the Great Dane, had a problem. A weird problem. He couldn't stop licking. His obsessive licking—of the sofa, the family's guests, even the floor—drove his owners and their guests crazy. These behaviors were peculiar and annoying, especially when non-dog-lovers came to call. They didn't care to be licked, thank you very much. Giant's licking obsession became so problematic that the poor dog had to be crated as soon as guests walked through the door.

These obsessive behaviors became so much a part of the dog that it seemed impossible to overcome. Eventually the vet offered a solution—a supplement that calmed the pup down. It didn't completely solve the problem but helped to some degree.

Maybe you can relate to Giant. Perhaps you've got habits—problems, concerns, worries—that plague you. You can't seem to let go of them, no matter how hard you try. You've given yourself over to the notion that things will never change, that you'll always struggle with the same issues. You just can't stop licking—er, worrying.

There's good news for you today! God can help you release those pains, those worries, those problems. He can help you "lick" those troubling habits and toss them to the curb. You can start fresh. Begin by writing down the things that are bothering you. Make a list. Then read the list aloud, saying the words, "Lord, today I give You _____." (Fill in the blank with the thing that is troubling you.)

God will take those things from you and handle them in His way, but you have to let go. You have to stop obsessing. Release them, then watch your heavenly Father work on your behalf.

Lord, today I choose to let go.
No more obsessing. No more fussing
and fretting. I extend my palms
and release those problems.
Take them, I pray, and show
me a better way.

AMEN.

21

Sniffing Out the Problem

The word of God is living and active, sharper than any two-edged sword, piercing to the division of soul and of spirit, of joints and of marrow, and discerning the thoughts and intentions of the heart.

HEBREWS 4:12 ESV

...

Ella had lived with seizures all of her life. For many years, medication kept them under control. But, as she approached her thirties, they seemed to get worse, not better.

With the help of a national organization, Ella adopted a service dog. Frankie—a yellow lab—alerted her when a seizure was coming. With his help, she was able to get herself to safety before trouble hit. No more hitting the floor when a seizure came. Ella was seated or lying down from the onset to avoid hitting her head or causing injury. Frankie's presence proved to be a lifesaver on multiple occasions.

Dogs have discernment. They can be trained to detect trouble. They can sniff it out before it even comes, which is remarkable if you think about it.

Did you realize you have built-in discernment as well? It's one of the many gifts of the Holy Spirit. He gives you the ability to discern when someone is up to no good, when they're about to take advantage of you. He helps you make decisions—about everything from your job to who you should marry. This amazing ability (to tell good from evil) is even more remarkable than a dog's ability to sniff out trouble before it hits.

Do you lean on God's discernment or follow after your own instincts? Are you really pausing and listening for His still, small voice before forging ahead or are you more inclined to take off at lightning speed and hope for the best?

Listen. Really listen. Then move as the Holy Spirit whispers direction in that still, small voice.

Lord, I'm listening. Please "grow" my discernment. I want my life to be the best it can be, and I know that depends on hearing and obeying Your voice. Help me with that, I pray.

AMEN.

Knee Jerking

A fool gives full vent to his spirit, but a wise man quietly holds it back. . . . Do you see a man who is hasty in his words? There is more hope for a fool than for him.

PROVERBS 29:11, 20 ESV

• • •

Lizzy awoke from a sound sleep as her German shepherd's deep barks reverberated across the bedroom.

"Hush, Bella!" Lizzy rolled over in the bed and pulled the covers up to her chin. "You're going to wake the neighbors."

Bella didn't seem to care about that. She knelt at the closed bedroom door and barked at an invisible something-or-another on the other side. On and on she went, her barks getting more animated with time.

It took a minute for Lizzy to realize what was going on. She had turned on the washing machine before getting into bed. It had just switched to the spin cycle, which had alerted Bella. The poor dog felt sure they were under attack.

"It's just the washer, honey. Calm down." Lizzy

spoke in her most soothing voice as she sat up in the bed. "You're going to wake the neighbors."

Bella didn't seem to understand. She continued to bark and bark until the spin cycle finally came to a halt.

Sometimes we're a little like Bella, aren't we? We hear something—a rumor, a false accusation, a story about someone we love—and we knee jerk. Before waiting for all of the evidence to come in we start barking. Our knee-jerk reactions are swift. Only one problem—they're not always appropriate.

When was the last time you knee jerked? Did you regret it afterward? God longs for you to sit a moment and assess the situation before reacting. Don't be like Bella. Pause and listen. Maybe, just maybe, it's just the washer switching to the spin cycle.

Lord, I'll confess: I'm a reactor. I knee jerk. . .a lot. Please forgive me for the times I've gotten ahead of You or misunderstood the circumstances. I'm sorry for the times I've falsely accused others or pointed fingers wrongly. Help me to take a deep breath and ask Your opinion before reacting, I pray.

AMEN.

23

Healing Touch

God shows his love for us in that while
we were still sinners, Christ died for us.

ROMANS 5:8 ESV

• • •

Dahlia stopped at her local animal shelter to drop off donations. While there, she peeked in the small dog room. The place was buzzing with people. They were in love with the puppies, the little female doxie, the chiweenie, and the Chihuahua. But no one, absolutely no one, was giving the little rat terrier (the one with major skin issues) a second glance. It was easy to see why. One look and you knew. . .this one was going to take time. And work. And gentleness. And a strong stomach.

Dahlia started talking to him and he responded to the soothing tone of her voice. Still, she was terrified to touch him. Eventually she opened the door to his crate and patted him on the head. It was all over after that. Thirty minutes later (with meds in hand and lengthy instructions about his daily care scribbled down) she carried him out of the shelter, wrapped in a towel.

When they arrived home Dahlia gave little Romeo a medicated bath then fed the underweight pup a hearty meal of chicken.

By the next morning the redness in his skin was greatly diminished. Dahlia was shocked. Another thing shocked her. . .he wanted to cuddle. Over the next few days, as his skin healed, he grew more and more cuddly.

Dahlia's heart was touched. She was so glad she had taken the risk to love him. As she patted that precious little head and let him lay it on her lap, she renewed her commitment to let him know how worthy of love he was.

Doesn't that sound just like God's love for us? He sees us in our ickiest state. Instead of saying, "I'll wait until she's cleaned up," He sweeps us into His arms and loves us so beautifully that we think we're already perfect in His sight. And the best thing is. . .we are perfect in His sight.

Thank You, Lord, for not waiting until I had my act together to love me. I'm so grateful that You adore me, in spite of my mess! I praise You for Your kindness, Father.

AMEN.

24

Don't Poke the Bear

A gentle answer turns away wrath, but a harsh word stirs up anger. The tongue of the wise adorns knowledge, but the mouth of the fool gushes folly.

PROVERBS 15:1–2 NIV

• • •

Winston loved to doze in the sunlight. On a warm, sunny afternoon the lazy Saint Bernard could most often be found on a cushioned bench in the fenced backyard, rolling back and forth between his back and his belly. He could remain in this position for hours on end, snoozing the day away and dreaming of lovely treats and tummy tickles.

Only one problem: His "awake" hours looked a bit different. Winston had the strange habit of awakening with a start, usually stirred by the sound of a neighbor dog barking or a car pulling into the driveway. The yapping would begin in earnest the moment he woke from his sleep. He would bare his teeth and come out swinging. Talk about waking up on the wrong side of the bed! What a grouch!

Some people are like that sleeping dog. You don't

want to poke them. If you do. . .watch out! They come flying at you like a swarm of mosquitos, stingers ready to do damage. They're easily provoked and quick to react.

What about you? Would people say you're a bear when you're poked? Do you come out of the gate, guns blazing? Or do you respond with a soft answer and avoid confrontation?

God has a solution for bears like that. His Word encourages us to answer with gentleness, to turn away wrath (anger). If you come out of the gate swinging, people will swing back. . .and things rarely end well.

Guard your tongue and you'll guard your life. Don't poke the bear. . .and don't be a bear. Learn to respond as Jesus would, with kindness, gentleness, and self-control.

Lord, I don't want to be known as a bear. Please temper my reactions (emphasis on "temper"). Guard my words. Rid me of the harsh ones, I pray, and place Your words of kindness on my tongue.

AMEN.

I HAVE FOUND THAT WHEN
YOU ARE DEEPLY TROUBLED,
THERE ARE THINGS YOU GET
FROM THE SILENT DEVOTED
COMPANIONSHIP OF A DOG
THAT YOU CAN GET FROM NO
OTHER SOURCE.

Doris Day

25

Safe in His Arms

The Lord your God is in your midst,
a mighty one who will save; He will rejoice over you
with gladness; He will quiet you by His love; He will
exult over you with loud singing.

ZEPHANIAH 3:17 ESV

• • •

There's nothing finer than a quiet afternoon curled up on the sofa with a pup in your lap. Cuddling, loving, scratching that little darling behind the ears. . .it brings comfort to both the dog and the owner. It doesn't cost a penny (it's definitely cheaper than therapy!), and it provides the perfect opportunity to show how much you care.

It's no wonder dogs are called man's best friends! They truly love to stick close and don't care what you're wearing, how you've fixed your hair, or what's on the agenda. Spending time in the presence of the one who cares for their every need is in their nature. There, half-awake, half-asleep, they have no concerns for their safety, no doubts about where the next meal is coming from, no reason to fear any would-be intruders. They're safe in their master's arms, completely relaxed, totally at home.

Whenever you spend time with the Lord, you're equally safe. There's nothing to fear as long as you're close to Him. In fact, cuddled up in His arms, you won't be thinking about the electric bill or the car payment. You'll stop fretting over that big decision to be made at work. You won't even be stirred up over the kids fighting. The Lord has you safely tucked under His wings and you're absolutely sure He's got everything covered. He's quieting you with His love. He's even rejoicing over you with singing. (Isn't that a lovely image?)

Don't let anything steal your time away from God. Where else can you go to find the answers—and the peace—you need?

Lord, I want to hang out with You today! When I'm with You, nothing else matters. I'm not hyper-focused on my problems or fretting over what's coming next. I'm completely relaxed, content to be Your child. Thank You for drawing me close, Father.

AMEN.

26

Jumping the Gate

*He jumped to his feet and began to walk.
Then he went with them into the temple courts,
walking and jumping, and praising God.*

ACTS 3:8 NIV

• • •

Nellie took excellent care of her sick little foster pup, Penny. She nursed her through a lengthy battle with kennel cough and kept her separated from the other dogs with the help of a baby gate. Several days into Penny's care the little pooch decided she was well enough to ditch her digs. The hyper canine took a flying leap over the baby gate and bounded through the living room, tail wagging merrily, as if to say, "You can't stop me now!"

"Looks like you're feeling better!" Nellie laughed and scratched the sweet pup behind the ears. "But I still need to keep you separated from the others, just in case you're contagious."

That turned out to be harder than she had imagined. Sweet Penny was feeling so much better that she refused to be held back. She kept jumping the baby gate, multiple times in a row. Nellie finally gave up. Looked like Penny was ready to get back to a normal life.

Can you relate to Penny's dilemma? When you're going through a "down" season (sickness or depression) you're fine to stay inside the gate. This is especially true when you're feeling defeated. But when God does a healing work in your life your faith is activated! Discouragement flees and you jump the gate back to normal living.

Don't let the cares of life keep you caged for too long. If you need help, ask for it. Spend time in God's presence and let Him heal you. Reach out to others for additional help. Then, with the faith of a hyper pup, leap that gate and get back to the land of the living.

Lord, I've jumped plenty of gates in my day, thanks to Your healing power. Thank You for the many, many times You've healed me—physically, emotionally, and psychologically. Living in freedom is so much better than being caged up!

AMEN.

27

Mutts

For everything God created is good, and nothing is to be rejected if it is received with thanksgiving.

I TIMOTHY 4:4 NIV

• • •

Julie didn't look like her friends. Most were trim and beautiful. She was petite, chubby, and, well, a little on the plain side. There were other differences, too. Many of her friends were happily married. Julie was still reeling from a recent divorce.

Her friends, for the most part, had wonderful, spacious homes, beautifully decorated, with all of the latest, trendiest electronics and décor. Julie's townhouse was very plain by comparison and not large enough to accommodate more than one or two guests at a time. Even her dog—a Heinz 57 shelter pup—didn't match up with their pedigree pooches. Not that Julie minded. She preferred her little mutt and wouldn't trade him for anything in the world. In fact, he helped get her through the rocky divorce.

Maybe you can relate to Julie. Maybe there are times you feel like your friends and coworkers are all pedigrees and you're a mutt. There's nothing special or beautiful about you, at least to your way of thinking. You look at your life—at the things you don't have—and you say, "How come everyone else has it better? Why wasn't I given a life of ease?"

The truth is, very few people come into this world with stellar situations. There aren't a lot of babies born with silver spoons in their mouths.

It's time to stop comparing yourself to others. Those friends love you, not because of how you look or where you live, but because you're you. Embrace your differences. Own them. Don't waste your time fretting over the life you're supposedly missing out on. God has given you an amazing life, right where you are (and exactly how you are). Praise Him for that life and then get back to the business of living!

Lord, I'm so thankful for my life. I might not have everything my friends have, but every single need is met. From this day forward I'll keep my focus on how You've blessed me, Father. My heart overflows with gratitude!

AMEN.

28

Back Away from the Bowl

You desire but do not have, so you kill. You covet but you cannot get what you want, so you quarrel and fight. You do not have because you do not ask God.

JAMES 4:2 NIV

• • •

Aussie, the Australian shepherd, was the picture-perfect pup—except at mealtime. Whenever her owner would set the bowl on the floor, Aussie would snarl and growl at the other dog, a toy poodle.

"Aussie, stop that," her owner would scold. "Be nice to Kiki."

But Aussie wouldn't let up until the meal was over. She was quite a bear at dinnertime, even threatening to bite Kiki if she passed by.

Frustrated, Aussie's owner separated the dogs at every meal. Doing so felt like putting a bandage on a gaping wound, but she had to protect poor Kiki from this would-be attacker.

There are a lot of people out there who behave

like Aussie. They want what they want and don't care how many people they have to take down to get it. They growl at anyone who comes close, as if to say, "This is mine. Leave it alone." They're so possessive of their things that they come across as stingy and selfish.

God didn't create His kids to be stingy. He placed generosity in your heart and hopes you'll utilize it. So, back away from the bowl. Let someone else eat for a change. Give others opportunities to have some of the things you desire for yourself. In other words, treat them the way you would want to be treated—generously, with genuine affection.

Lord, thank You for the reminder that I shouldn't be selfish or stingy. It's not always easy to remember in the moment. I have a tendency to hold tight to what's mine. Help me loosen my grip, Father, and back away from the bowl so that others can enjoy the bounty too.

AMEN.

29

Love and Respect for the Elderly

Stand up in the presence of the aged, show respect for the elderly and revere your God. I am the LORD.

LEVITICUS 19:32 NIV

• • •

The little dog shivering in the back of the crate was completely blind and nearly deaf. The poor tiny darling was nearly fifteen years old and had a mammary tumor, to boot. Just the sight of her broke Hannah's heart. There was no logical reason to adopt this unhealthy senior citizen from the shelter that day. Hannah had come in looking for a younger, healthier dog, after all. But, as she stared into the miniature dachshund's face, she had no choice. Gigi needed someone who could offer love, care, and compassion for however many days, weeks, or months she had left, and Hannah would be the one to give it, no matter how difficult.

Hannah devoted herself to the little dog. She did her best to "show" the pup around her house and small backyard. Gigi settled in fine but required a lot of extensive care and attention. The precious little senior only lived a few weeks before cancer took its toll, but they were weeks filled with love and tender care. Tears poured from Hannah's eyes on the day Gigi passed away. She had to conclude: it had been worth it to provide the care the little dog needed.

Gigi's story is a gentle reminder that there are many, many senior citizens out there who've been overlooked. Many require additional love and care. They don't need to be abandoned. Today, why not visit an elderly neighbor or perhaps take cookies to a nursing home? When you drop them off, don't just leave them and run. Stay. Talk to some of the residents. Let them fill your ears with stories of years gone by.

The Word of God is clear that we're to care for the elderly, to show them love and respect. This is one of the finest ways to honor God, by caring for the seniors in your life.

Lord, I appreciate the reminder to care for the elderly. I know it means a lot to You and it means a lot to me, too. Show me who I can minister to today, Father.

AMEN.

30

Leap Me Not into Temptation

Watch and pray so that you will not fall into temptation. The spirit is willing, but the flesh is weak.

MATTHEW 26:41 NIV

· · ·

Olivia pulled what was left of the red velvet cake out of the refrigerator and wrapped it in a small trash bag. When she returned from the store she'd toss it into the trash can outside. Right now, it was safe on the kitchen counter.

Imagine her surprise a short time later when Olivia arrived home to find the red velvet cake missing and the bag completely shredded on the floor. She searched until she located her beagle, Daisy. The usually energetic pup was hiding behind a chair, looking ill. Very ill.

"Tell me you didn't. . ." Olivia knelt down and saw the red velvet cake crumbs all over the dog's face. The little vixen even smelled like red velvet cake. "How in the world did you get onto the kitchen counter?"

She stared at the layout of the open living room and kitchen and realized the back of the sofa was just a couple of feet away from the edge of the counter. So that's how Daisy had done it. The pooch had taken a flying leap and made herself a feast of the cake.

Olivia had no choice. Red velvet cakes were made of chocolate and red dye—both of which are harmful to dogs. She rushed her to the vet's office where the vet made ready work of getting the cake out of Daisy's tummy. Talk about a messy (and expensive) process.

That's how temptation is. It looks so good. It smells so good. It tastes so good. But there's always a price to pay. Loss of health. Loss of relationships. Loss of respect from family members and friends. Loss of respect for yourself. A long road back to where you began. Whew. That's a lot, just for one indiscretion.

Don't take the leap. Leave that red velvet cake alone! There's no point in giving in when you know the price will be so high. God will help you, if you ask Him.

Lord, I'm grateful for the reminder not to take the leap. It's just not worth it. Thanks for that reminder. I'll stay put, Father.

AMEN.

31

Runaways

The word of the LORD came to Jonah son of Amittai:
"Go to the great city of Nineveh and preach against it,
because its wickedness has come up before me." But
Jonah ran away from the LORD and headed for Tarshish.
He went down to Joppa, where he found a ship bound
for that port. After paying the fare, he went aboard and
sailed for Tarshish to flee from the LORD.

JONAH 1:1–3 NIV

. . .

Pepito, the Pomeranian, had to be watched closely.
Every time the front door opened, he tried to bolt out
into the street. Many times he managed, and his owner, Michelle, took off after him. But Pepito was fast!
He could make it all the way down the block before
Michelle was even halfway there. And talk about yapping! The little Pomeranian would bark at everyone
he met along the way. Once Michelle caught up with
him, she found herself apologizing—to the postal
worker, the next-door neighbor, even a delivery man.
What a little rascal.

One day Pepito snuck out when Michelle wasn't

looking. Hours went by. Michelle and her children combed the streets, looking for him. They were just about to give up hope when one of the neighbors posted on the neighborhood site that Pepito had been found at a nearby park. Michelle was relieved—and humiliated.

Pepito isn't really all that different from the prodigals you know, is he? They do the right thing until they're given the opportunity to do the wrong one. Then they bolt. They start hanging out with the wrong friends. They try alcohol, cigarettes, drugs. You do your best to drag them back home but have to make apologies along the way. It's a tough life, chasing after someone who doesn't want to stay put.

It's time to put the ultimate tracking device on your prodigal—prayer. You can't always chase him—or her—down, but God can. Pray, do what you can, and leave the rest to the One who sees and knows exactly where that runaway is.

Thank You for the reminder that I can't always rescue the runaways, Lord. I leave that up to You from now on.

AMEN.

32

Blessings Shower Down

*Love is patient, love is kind. It does not
envy, it does not boast, it is not proud.*

I CORINTHIANS 13:4 NIV

• • •

Kendra was whipping up some frosting for a birthday cake for her daughter. She added the powdered sugar while the mixer blades were whirring, and white puffs of sugar shot straight into the air and flew to the ground below, coating everything in sight. Including the little Welsh corgi at her feet.

Kendra glanced down and discovered Luna's back was completely covered in the white powdery mist! Luna was absolutely giddy at her good fortune. The smell of sugar was everywhere and she could hardly wait to taste it. Talk about a blessing!

Now, dogs have a unique problem that humans don't. They can't reach their own backs. Had she really received this sugary blessing, only to find it out of reach? What a sad pooch! There was really no way to clean off the sugar, short of rolling around on the rug.

No problem! Kendra's other dog, Nova, showed

up moments later and went to work, cleaning Luna's back. He had a blast, licking off that sweetness. Poor Luna! She got the powdered sugar shower; Nova got the benefits.

How many times has that happened in your life? It happens all the time! You come so close to receiving a blessing, only to lose it in the eleventh hour to someone else. How sad, to watch as others reap the benefits while you go without.

We have two choices when we face near-miss blessings. We can either grow bitter or we can hang around at the Master's feet to experience the next overflow. It is coming, you know. He's got blessings in abundance for all of His kids. We've just got to be like Luna, ready to lap it up when the moment comes.

I don't always take the prize, Lord, but I'm hanging out at Your feet regardless! It's my favorite place to be—not because of what You have to offer, but because of who You are. You are my Father and I am Your child.

How grateful I am!

AMEN.

EVER CONSIDER WHAT OUR
DOGS MUST THINK OF US?
I MEAN, HERE WE COME BACK
FROM A GROCERY STORE
WITH THE MOST AMAZING
HAUL, CHICKEN, PORK,
HALF A COW. THEY MUST
THINK WE'RE THE GREATEST
HUNTERS ON EARTH!

Anne Tyler

33

Buzzing with Anticipation

*It is fine to be zealous, provided the purpose is good,
and to be so always, not just when I am with you.*

GALATIANS 4:18 NIV

. . .

"You need to crate him when you leave the house,
honey," Beth's husband said. "That dog is tearing
up everything!"

"I know, I know. But she's too big for the crate. I
need to buy a new one. I'll do it soon, I promise."

With that excuse fresh on her lips, Beth headed
out to the grocery store. She was only gone for an
hour and a half, but when she arrived home she was
mortified to see that the family's dog—a shepherd
mix they'd named Bambina—had managed to topple
the coffee cart. Covering the floor were tea bags, lots
and lots of teabags. A couple looked as if they'd been
chewed. Loose tea covered the room, along with
scraps of coffee creamer packets.

Bambina was particularly crazy that night—rac-
ing around the house, crashing into things, knocking
lamps and books over. No doubt the pooch was caf-

feinated. It eventually wore off, but Beth had learned her lesson. She bought a new crate and put Bambina in it every time she left the house after that.

Maybe you can relate to Bambina's zeal. You get hyped up about something (an idea for a project at work, perhaps, or a terrific idea for the women's ministry at church). You buzz from here to there, bumping into all sorts of folks with your enthusiasm. Only, your excitement isn't matched by those around you. They just want you to calm down, to stay in your corner, to listen to their ideas, not act on your own. Ugh! Don't they see that you've got value? You can accomplish a lot, if they'll just let you.

It's not easy to contain our zeal when we have ideas, but sometimes it's necessary. Just take a deep breath, curb that enthusiasm, and wait for the proper time. God will let you shine at just the right moment.

Lord, I don't always want to wait! I've got such amazing ideas. I hate to see them tabled before I even have a chance. But I'll trust Your timing, Father. You'll let me shine when the time is right.

AMEN.

34

Change, Change, Change

*Jesus Christ is the same
yesterday and today and forever.*

HEBREWS 13:8 NIV

...

They looked like German shepherd puppies. Sort of. So, Cora wasn't surprised that the shelter had labeled the three six-week-old littermates as such.

When she agreed to take them on as fosters Cora had no idea that two of the three would turn out to look more like huskies than shepherds. And the little black pup, the one with a white stripe down her face? Turned out she was the only real shepherd in the bunch, though her hair changed from black to brown as she grew. . .and grew. . .and grew. By the time she was six months old the five-pound pup was fifty pounds and bore no resemblance to the once-tiny puppy. The transformation startled Cora. Talk about a radical change!

Maybe you've been there. You've adopted an adorable little puppy and watched it grow into an oversized dog that looked nothing like the pup you once knew.

The process (and outcome) can be rather shocking.

Life is like that sometimes too. You think you can predict something will happen, and. . .bam. Something else happens. You find yourself in the middle of a work-related debacle and you have a pretty good idea how it will pan out. . .then the story takes a twist. You're sure about a person's godly character, and then. . .oops. They let you down. You're taken aback and unsure of how to handle the change.

Life doesn't always turn out the way you think it will. People aren't always who you think they'll be. Situations aren't always what they appear. But there is One who is always and forever the same. Jesus Christ is the same yesterday, today, and forever. He never changes. He'll never let you down. If He said it, He'll do it.

I'm so glad You won't let me down, Jesus. I never have to wonder. I never have to fret. You're consistently loving, good, and kind to me, and I'm so grateful.

AMEN.

35

Digging Holes

*We know that in all things God works
for the good of those who love Him, who have
been called according to His purpose.*

ROMANS 8:28 NIV

· · ·

"Buster, what have you done? You've ruined my beautiful yard!"

Kelly couldn't help but groan as she looked out over her once-lovely backyard. The scene in front of her looked somewhat apocalyptic. Whole sections of grass were missing. The garden was filled with holes, some big enough to do damage to her ankles, should she accidentally step in them. The rocks lining the garden were spread around the yard in various places, and the small solar lanterns along the walkway had been pulled up and broken.

The lanterns weren't the only thing broken. Kelly's heart broke in two as she surveyed the mess. Why, oh why, had she said yes to this massive dog? He was more than she or her yard could handle. The destruction was really wearing her down. Should she admit defeat and re-home him? Or, would an obedience class do the trick?

It's easy to feel sorry for Kelly, isn't it? To have some-one—or in this case, something—destroy your hard work is agonizing.

Do you wonder if that's how God feels sometimes? He took the time to create us, to craft us in His image, and we make a mess of things. We get caught up with the wrong people. We dabble in things we shouldn't. We consume the wrong foods and create health problems for ourselves.

The truth is, we're a hot mess. We're just like Buster, digging up the yard. Instead of groaning as He surveys the damage, God gently lifts us up, brushes us off, and says, "I forgive you. I love you anyway."

Then He puts us through obedience school. We receive a bit of life training from the Master Trainer. Even-tually we learn the lessons and our behavior changes for the better. But how good of God to keep on loving us in the meantime. (He has no re-homing policy! When God adopts us, it's a forever deal.)

I'm grateful You've been willing to clean up my messes, Lord. I've made so many. Thank You for forgiving me and offering guidance so I can do better next time.

AMEN.

36

When Hope Seems Lost

Guide me in Your truth and teach me, for You are God my Savior, and my hope is in You all day long.

PSALM 25:5 NIV

• • •

Samantha stared down at her little bichon frise, Cotton, and whispered a prayer. "God, I know she's in bad shape. It doesn't look like she's going to make it. But I'm going to pray anyway. You can heal her, Lord, if You choose to. It's going to take a miracle, but I know You excel at those."

The little dog struggled to catch her breath before another round of coughing hit. The poor darling was struggling with double pneumonia, a secondary infection that now threatened to take her life. Burning up with fever, she could barely lift her head.

Samantha continued to pray as she gave Cotton a breathing treatment. She managed to grind up an antibiotic tablet and mix it with water to put into a syringe, then she pried the little dog's lips apart to run the liquid down her throat. This battle to keep the pup going was taking a toll on Samantha, but she refused to give up. Cotton deserved all the care she could offer.

It took days, but the little dog's temperature finally started to come down and her lungs began to recover. She began to eat and take more than a sip of water at a time.

Within a week, she was healthy enough to take out for a walk. Samantha kept a watchful eye out for more symptoms, but (thank goodness) they did not appear. It looked like the crisis was over. Cotton was going to make it.

If you've walked a loved one through a near-death experience, you know how touch-and-go things can get. It's not always easy to keep your faith. But perhaps you are on the brink of your miracle at the very moment when you feel like giving up. Keep hoping. Keep praying. Trust your Miracle Worker.

Lord, I know You can work miracles and there are times in my life (and the lives of those I love) where a miracle is our only hope. Thank You for intervening at just the right time, Father. I choose to put my trust in You.

AMEN.

37

An Ounce of Prevention

Do your best to present yourself to God as one approved, a worker who does not need to be ashamed and who correctly handles the word of truth.

II TIMOTHY 2:15 NIV

• • •

Just one pill a month. That's all it takes to prevent a dog from getting heartworm, a deadly disease that kills one out of every two hundred dogs per year. One pill a month works as a preventative, offering protection not just from heartworms but from other common parasites, as well. One pill a month can make the difference between life and death. So, pet owners around the globe are offering their dogs and cats this wonder drug in the hopes that Fido and Fifi can live happier, healthier lives. Sure, the medicine costs a little money, but it's nothing compared to the cost of heartworm treatment.

Maybe you've heard the old adage, "An ounce of prevention is worth a pound of cure." In almost every scenario you will face in this life, the "cure" is a lot more work than the prevention. Managing type 2 diabetes, for instance. Or dealing with a grown child who can't hold down a job because he was never made to do anything for himself. What about this one: taking care of a blown engine in a car after letting the oil run out. The prevention would've been easier. Far easier.

God's Word acts as a preventative. When you take it daily it can prevent all sorts of harder-to-deal-with issues like hopelessness, anger, frustration, bitterness, and so on. An ounce of prevention (reading your Bible and praying) is worth a pound of cure (dealing with the effects of despair).

Reading the Word will keep you on the offense instead of the defense. It will build you into a strong woman, one capable of conquering many foes. So, the next time you're tempted to step away from your Bible, remember—that daily ounce of prevention can lead to a very full and happy life.

Lord, I'm glad You've reminded me that reading the Word is a preventative for the many, many spiritual ailments I might otherwise face. I want to be on the offense, Father, not the defense. So, I'll read my Bible and stick close to You.

AMEN.

38

Can't We All Just Get Along?

If it is possible, as far as it depends on you,
live at peace with everyone.

ROMANS 12:18 NIV

• • •

Jessica worked at a doggy daycare four afternoons a week. For the most part she loved her job. But there were days when the chaos was more than she could handle.

On a particularly rough afternoon she found herself taking care of six dogs in one small play area. The bullmastiff wasn't bothering any of the other pups. He was content to lie in the sun and rest. That cocker spaniel, however? She hadn't stopped barking since her owner dropped her off. And then there was the lab puppy. He just wanted to play with everyone, including the bullmastiff, who wanted to be left alone. Factor in the rowdy Doberman, the feisty Chihuahua and the stubborn Pekingese, and Jessica had her hands full.

It's not so different with people, really. Whenever

you get a lot of different personalities together at once, it can be tough for everyone to get along. Maybe you've experienced this in a board meeting at church or hanging out with a group of girlfriends. Every circle of friends has the pushy one. There's always one who's hyper and ready to have a good time. Every circle has the stubborn friend, the feisty friend, and so on.

Why did God make people with such distinct personalities? Perhaps He wants to challenge us, to mold us into His image. Maybe the goal in making us all different was to show the different facets of His personality. (We're made in His image, after all.)

Instead of making a big deal out of your differences, take the time to focus on what you have in common with your friends. Get to know the various personality types and love each other through the differences.

Lord, I'm grateful for my friends,
no matter how different they are.
It's not always easy to keep the chaos
at a minimum, but my friendships mean
so much to me, Father. They're worth
fighting for.
AMEN.

39

Scraps from the Table

"Lord," she replied, "even the dogs under the table eat the children's crumbs."

MARK 7:28 NIV

• • •

Misty fed her shih tzu table scraps from her own meals. Apollo swallowed them down, tail wagging. Kibble from a bag? No thank you. He preferred nibbles of salty steak, chunks of deep-fried chicken, and even special treats like the occasional french fry or cookie. Misty loved pampering her little baby and enjoyed seeing him happy. It warmed her heart. So she didn't see any problem with the table scraps. Until the little pooch was diagnosed with chronic pancreatitis. Turned out, the high-fat, high-carb diet was too much for Apollo to handle. Years of bad food had finally taken a toll.

To turn his health around, the vet put Apollo on special easy-to-digest food with a lower calorie content. Used to getting his own way, the dog staged a protest. He simply wouldn't eat until Misty fed him the usual fare. She gave in from time to time but did her best to stick to the plan. After all, she didn't want Apollo to suffer.

The little pooch didn't realize that what seemed better (the table scraps) was ultimately worse for him. The same can be said about many of our decisions. We want what we want and we're sure it's going to be great. Then we get what we wanted and it doesn't turn out to be so great. We stubbornly hold on to the idea that our plans will bring us the most success. We don't always realize that God has a better way.

Maybe it's time to trade in our idea of "great" for God's idea of "greater."

Don't settle. Table scraps might be tempting, but they're just that. . .scraps. God has a feast prepared for you. How can you enjoy it with a tummy full of scraps?

Lord, I'm not willing to survive on scraps anymore. What You've got for me is so much better! It might seem like a sacrifice at times, but I want what's best for me. Show me where tweaks need to be made, Father.
I want Your very best.

AMEN.

40

Managing the Stairs

Therefore, since we are surrounded by such a great cloud of witnesses, let us throw off everything that hinders and the sin that so easily entangles. And let us run with perseverance the race marked out for us.

HEBREWS 12:1 NIV

* * *

Hailey's new puppy was a feisty, fun little thing. The chubby golden retriever bounded around the living room and kitchen running into all kinds of other things. But every time Hailey would go upstairs, the little boy would start howling.

"It's okay, Geno!" Hailey called out. "C'mon up."

The pup stood at the bottom of the staircase gazing up, up, up, but was unwilling to budge. No doubt the sheer size of the staircase intimidated him.

Hailey walked to the bottom step and sat down. She patted the stair with her hand until the dog caught on. He gingerly made the step up.

"There you go, honey! You've got the idea!" Hailey scooted up a couple of steps and kept patting until the little dog attempted the climb.

It took some time, but Geno finally made it to the top of the stairs. Getting down the first couple of times was tough, but he eventually conquered the downward motions too.

Maybe you've walked a mile in Geno's (proverbial) shoes. You've wanted to step out in faith, to conquer something big, but you see that staircase looming above you and you're scared. Remember, you can take it one step at a time. Just in case you're worried you won't make it, remember the millions of believers who've gone before you. Moses, David, Paul, Timothy. . .they all started at the bottom of the staircase, just like you. These spiritual giants accomplished great things for the kingdom of God and so will you. So, what's holding you back? Take that first step, girl!

Lord, I'm emboldened by the stories of those who've gone before me. They made the climb and did great things for You. I want to do the same, so here I go, Father! I'm taking that first step!

AMEN.

IT WAS ME.
I LET THE DOGS OUT.

Anonymous

41

He's Got it Covered

My God will meet all your needs according to the riches of His glory in Christ Jesus.

PHILIPPIANS 4:19 NIV

• • •

Joy paced the lobby of the vet's office, sick with worry. Her miniature dachshund had lost the use of his back legs. According to the vet, a disc in his back had gone out, causing instant paralysis. Now at a specialty clinic, a neurosurgeon had just given Joy the bad news—Copper would have to have spinal surgery. Immediately. If he didn't, the prognosis would be grim. He would permanently lose control of his bladder and bowels and would never walk again. Worse still, he would be in pain.

It had to be done. No doubt about that. But. . .how? She swallowed hard as she thought about the cost. Nearly three thousand dollars. . .for a dog? Would her friends think she'd lost her mind? It seemed an impossible price to pay, especially being on such a tight budget. But, what else could she do? She loved that little dog and couldn't bear to see him suffer.

Joy reached for her credit card and paid the receptionist so that Copper could have his life-saving surgery. It would take a few months to pay off, but her little pup was worth it.

Maybe you've been in Joy's place. An unexpected crisis has knocked you off your feet financially. The washer went out. Your car's timing belt broke. The AC unit went bust smack-dab in the middle of the summer.

Things happen. But remember, God is a need-meeter. He knows what you need even before you ask and He's already made provision for it. So, don't fret when things go wrong. Keep your faith! Take joy in the fact that the Lord's already got it covered.

Lord, I trust You, even in the lean seasons. I get scared sometimes. I'll confess it. But I will stand on the promises I find in Your Word. You will make provision for all of my needs and I'm so grateful.

AMEN.

42

Old Dog, New Tricks

Do not be conformed to this world, but be transformed by the renewing of your mind, that you may prove what is that good and acceptable and perfect will of God.

ROMANS 12:2 NKJV

• • •

Maybe you've heard the old expression, "You can't teach an old dog new tricks." It might make for a clever saying, but it's not true. Anyone can change—at any stage of life—if they're willing.

You might debate that point. You might look at an elderly father who's given himself over to alcoholism and say, "There's just no way. We lost him years ago. No point in even going there." Or you might look at a friend who holds staunchly to her opinion that there is no God and you might quip, "That one will never come around. Whatever you do, don't start a debate with her!" Maybe you look at a rebellious teenager and say, "That's just his personality. He was born that way. He's just like his dad. I can't expect him to change."

Don't give up! God can tug on hearts. He can use circumstances to nudge people—even impossible people—in His direction. And He can use you to help. So, don't close your eyes (or your heart) to the ones who seem impossible. Sure, many are hard cases. Very hard. And yes, you'll probably get hurt a time or two if you keep reaching out or speaking truth. But don't focus on the here and now. Focus on how good it's going to feel when that person finally comes around. What a glorious day that will be.

Old dogs can learn new tricks. They can.

Are there any new tricks you need to learn?

Lord, I have to confess, I've given up on a few friends and family members. I don't even remember to pray for them anymore. They seem too far away from You, too lost to redeem. But You love hard cases, Father. Thank You for the reminder that it's not too late.

AMEN.

43

Out for a Walk

Follow God's example, therefore, as dearly loved children and walk in the way of love, just as Christ loved us and gave Himself up for us as a fragrant offering and sacrifice to God.

EPHESIANS 5:1–2 NIV

• • •

There are days when you simply don't want to get out of bed. Life is too overwhelming. You can't bear the thought of exerting any energy. Not today. Not with so many problems looming.

Then that great big lump of a dog sticks his nose in your face.

"Hey, you!" he hollers without saying a word. "Get up! I need to go out!"

And so, you drag yourself from the bed and get dressed to take him out for a walk. Before long you're waving at a neighbor, the one who's going through chemotherapy. You pause to ask her how she's doing. As you head back out, you notice the flowers blooming in another neighbor's front yard. Wow! Spring has sprung and you almost missed it! Your pup tugs on the leash, his gait faster than before. You rush to keep up.

The postal worker passes by in his truck and you give him a nod, then shift your gaze to the work being done on your friend's roof. Why didn't she tell you she was getting a new roof? Oh, right. Because you missed her last call and hadn't taken the time to call back. You stop off at her house and she invites you in for coffee. Before long you're laughing and talking. . .about anything and everything.

There's life outside the walls of your house. All you have to do is get out there and enjoy it. Toss those hermit tendencies. Bask in the sunshine. Drink in the fresh air. Enjoy the flowers. Wave to the people. Don't get so caught up in your own little bubble that you forget to enjoy what's all around you.

Lord, I'll confess, I'm prone to stay in my bubble. I don't pay much attention to what's going on around me, even in my own neighborhood. Show me how to be a friend to those close by, and help me see that life is worth living, even if it means I have to step out of my comfort zone.

AMEN.

44

Stay

You make known to me the path of life;
You will fill me with joy in your presence,
with eternal pleasures at Your right hand.

PSALM 16:11 NIV

• • •

Teaching a dog to sit is one thing. Teaching him to stay is quite another. Dogs will sit for a treat. But. . .staying? That's a little harder. Patience doesn't come naturally to most breeds. They'd rather be running and playing in the yard than sitting still, eyes focused on the prize.

God has a difficult time getting His kids to stay put too. We're so antsy sometimes! He says, "Linger in My presence," and we say, "But, Lord. . .I've got plans today!" He says, "Get in the Bible. Search My truths!" and we say, "Sure, Father! I'll read a verse or two but I don't really have time for much more." He says, "Guard yourself! Don't wander too far from My commands!" and we say, "Can't I just hang out with this one friend? She won't pull me too far away from You, just a little." We just can't seem to stay, no matter how many times or ways He calls.

"Staying" implies a passage of time. It also implies extreme focus. When a dog "stays," his gaze is on you. It never leaves. He's not released until you give him the word. Then he bounds. . .where? Not away from you, but toward you. You release him and he runs straight into your arms.

God wants you to learn a lesson from your pup. Linger. Stay. Enjoy His presence. Stay close to His truths. Stay close to His heart. Stay close to His Word. Stay close in prayer. Stay close to the body of Christ. Stay near those who can build you up. Stay committed to your relationship with Him.

Stay.

It's not just a command for pups.

I'll stay, Lord! I won't leave You. I'll remain close in every way I can—from my time with You to my choice of friends. When You release me, I'll run straight to Your arms, Father.

AMEN.

45

Rescue the Perishing

The LORD who rescued me from the paw of the lion and the paw of the bear will rescue me from the hand of this Philistine.

I SAMUEL 17:37 NIV

• • •

You're scrolling the newsfeed of your favorite social media app when a picture stops you cold. A dog in the shelter, scheduled to be euthanized within hours. Your heart skips a beat. You stare and stare at that forlorn face, wishing you could do something. But you're already up to your eyeballs in pets at the moment and the house can't hold another.

So, you share the post. And you're relieved, an hour or so later, to see that someone has stepped up. Whew! That precious pup has been rescued. And you feel good that you played a role in it.

God is in the rescuing business, too. He doesn't need a newsfeed to see who's at risk. A quick glance and He can tell who's not going to make it without help.

So He sends people like you to the rescue. Friends with broad shoulders. Coworkers with listening ears.

Family members with an extra room to house a single mom and her kids. He sends you to make a difference, to rescue the perishing before they reach the end.

Sure, it feels good to rescue a pup but it feels even better to make a lasting difference in the lives of people you meet. You can't rescue everyone, but you can do your part. Send monthly support to a child in poverty. Give to your local homeless shelter. Support your church's various outreach ministries. Make sure the missionaries you love have what they need. Tend to the elderly. Take care of the sick.

In other words, be like Jesus.

Lord, I care so deeply about those in need. Please give me creative ways to reach out to those who need help. I don't want to enable but I do want to help. Thank You for opening my eyes to their needs, Father.

AMEN.

An Eternal Paw Print

*We will not hide them from their children,
but tell to the coming generation the glorious deeds
of the LORD, and his might, and the wonders that
he has done.*

PSALM 78:4 ESV

• • •

Kassy had the privilege of loving her little Yorkie, Sasha, for fifteen years. For the most part, she was a healthy dog, even in her later years. Then one day something went terribly wrong. Sasha wouldn't come out from under the bed. Kassy knelt down to coax her out but could tell the pup was lethargic. When she picked her up it was obvious the little dog was burning up with fever.

Kassy rushed Sasha to the animal hospital. After a thorough examination, the vet offered a grim diagnosis: heart failure. "Not much we can do."

The words left Kassy reeling. She left the vet's office with a bagful of meds and a list of instructions for Sasha's care. But by the next day the poor little dog was much worse off than before. It was clear the precious dog only had a matter of hours to live.

It wrecked Kassy to lose her friend. When the vet offered to have Sasha's paw print made, Kassy jumped at the opportunity. For years after losing Sasha she would look at that print and remember—the hours spent side by side on the sofa cuddling. The years of taking walks together through the neighborhood. The joys, the pains. . .she remembered it all. That little paw print served as a reminder of the legacy.

Have you ever pondered what sort of legacy you will leave when you're gone? Will those who remain remember how you loved them, how you cared for those in need, how you loved Jesus completely? You have an opportunity with each passing day to build on that legacy you'll one day leave behind.

What honor you will bring to your heavenly Father with a life well-lived! What a lovely paw print!

Father, I want to leave a legacy. I want others to remember how I loved You and how I loved them. Help me keep that in mind every day, Lord.

AMEN.

47

Deep Sleep

*In peace I will lie down and sleep, for you alone,
LORD, make me dwell in safety.*

PSALM 4:8 NIV

• • •

Have you ever watched a dog drift off to sleep? He
s-t-r-e-t-c-h-e-s, then settles down at his master's feet,
finding a comfortable position. Within seconds he
dozes off without a care in the world. Nothing matters, as long as they are close together. That pup can
sleep in perfect peace, never stirring.

The same is true when we put our head to the pil-
low at night. We have nothing to fear. All concerns
can be pushed aside. Our Master is right there, just a
breath away. He's tucked us in, easing all worries, and
longs for us to get the rest we need. (And getting a
great night's sleep is critical for good health, after all.)

What about you? How are your sleep habits? Do
you have a hard time drifting off? Are the cares and
concerns of life weighing you down? If so, then picture
yourself handing them to the Lord before you even
climb into bed at night. He can handle them, after all.

And He doesn't even need your help to do so.

Think about that for a moment. For eight solid hours, you're not in control. . .of anything. You hand over the reins to the One who created you, who cares more about you than you do yourself. During those hours you don't fret over what's going on at work or that hurtful thing a friend said to you. You're at the complete mercy of your Master.

That's how your pup feels, too. He's completely at ease, knowing you will keep him safe. What a lovely, precious image.

Father, I love my sleep time! That moment when I doze off is so holy, for it's when I hand over the reins completely. Thank You for giving me sweet sleep. Thank You for watching over me when I'm not awake to watch over myself. Most of all, thank You for being such a good, good Father, One who truly loves me—asleep or awake.

AMEN.

48

Facing the Big Dogs

Be strong and courageous. Do not be afraid or terrified because of them, for the LORD your God goes with you; He will never leave you nor forsake you.

DEUTERONOMY 31:6 NIV

• • •

Teeny, the teacup Chihuahua, was a little intimidated by the neighbor's Doberman. To her, he looked like a monstrous thing that could snap her up in one bite. The Dobie, Brutus, was as tame as could be, a real softie. He wanted nothing more than to play. But nothing could convince Teeny to trust him. Whenever he would peer at her through the slats in the fence the hairs on her back would stand straight up and she would bark in her tiny yappy voice. He backed away from the fence, perhaps wondering if that tiny little monster might take him down.

Maybe you've faced a few Brutuses in your life. They stood like mighty Goliaths in front of you, barking until your hands trembled and your heart raced. You were sure they were there to destroy you. Those moments can be terrifying!

But, take heart! Sometimes they're not really giants at all. They're softies, like Brutus. But when you do face a real giant—a cancer diagnosis, a broken marriage, a job loss—it's important to remember what David, the shepherd boy, did. He squared his shoulders, looked that giant in the eye, and then spoke words of faith over his situation. In other words, he didn't let the giant intimidate him. Then he gathered five smooth stones and laid that giant to rest, once and for all.

Don't let the big dogs scare you. Some are real, sure, but most of them are just peeking at you through the slats in the fence, wishing you'd come over to play.

Lord, I won't let the big dogs get me down. My knees won't knock when I see them coming. I'll assess them, ascertain whether they're really an enemy or just a very large friend—then respond with the faith of young David.

AMEN.

WHEN AN 85 POUND MAMMAL LICKS YOUR TEARS AWAY, AND THEN TRIES TO SIT ON YOUR LAP, IT'S HARD TO FEEL SAD.

Kristan Higgins

49

Fetch

Do not merely listen to the word, and so deceive yourselves. Do what it says.

JAMES 1:22 NIV

• • •

Courtney marveled at her dog's fascination with the game of fetch. The long-legged whippet loved to chase the ball all the way across the yard and then return it to her owner, over and over again. Sometimes the game went on for an hour or more. Even then Courtney had to coax the pup into taking a break.

Maybe you've got a similar situation at your house. Your dog loves to take what you toss out to him and can't wait to return it to you. Maybe he loves the smile on your face when he offers that ball to you as a gift.

Fetch and return. Fetch and return. It's a godly principle, if you really stop to think about it. There are certain aspects of our walk with God that are reminiscent of this game we play with our dogs. The Lord tosses out the principles in His Word—we fetch them and bring them back to Him with our obedience to them. He tosses out a specific call on our lives, a call to do something significant for Him—we fetch it and bring it back to Him by accepting the call and stepping out in faith. He tosses an instruction to help a person a need—we fetch it and bring it back to Him by reaching out a hand to help the one who needs us.

So, what has God tossed your way lately? Did you latch onto it or were you afraid you wouldn't have the stamina or the talent to see it through? It's time to step out in faith, woman of God, and fetch what He's tossing. The Lord is waiting for you to bring it back to Him as a gift.

Lord, I get it! You've given me so many things—Your Word, opportunities, blessings, and so on. You don't want me to sit on them. I'm to do something magnificent with them. I won't let fear stop me. From now on i'm acting on what You've placed in my hands. Thank You, Father!

AMEN.

50

The Spot Next to You

Give all your worries and cares to God,
for He cares about you.

I PETER 5:7 NLT

• • •

Linda arrived home after a long, hard day at work. She swallowed down the burger and fries she'd picked up at the fast food place and then plopped down on the sofa and put her feet up. Her Jack Russell terrier, Jax, decided to join her. He jumped up onto the sofa and took the spot next to her.

He didn't say a word. (Obviously.) She didn't say a word. They just sat together, enjoying the silence that hovered in the air between them. Linda eventually reached for the remote control and flipped on the television. She wasn't particularly interested in the show she chose but kept the TV playing in the background while she petted Jax and lost herself to her thoughts.

Before long, the cares of the day began to subside. The soothing motion of stroking the pup had a calming effect on her. In fact, Linda began to wonder how her friends who weren't dog owners managed to get through their rough patches without the help of a canine. After an hour or two of resting with the pup at her side, Linda got so relaxed that she almost dozed off.

In many ways, that's how God calms us down. He takes His position right next to us. His very presence is soothing, confirming. He gently eases away the tensions of the day until we are relaxed and still.

No matter what you're going through today, give your worries and cares to the Lord. Allow Him to get close enough to calm you. He has your best interest at heart and wants nothing more than to offer a comforting touch.

Lord, I'll save You the best seat, right next to me. You're the only one who can truly rid me of the stresses of the day. You comfort me, even when I'm wound up over a problem at work or a relational issue. Praise You, Father, for Your gentle care.

AMEN.

LIVE YOUR FAITH

Dear Friend,

This book was prayerfully crafted with you, the reader, in mind—every word, every sentence, every page—was thoughtfully written, designed, and packaged to encourage you...right where you are this very moment. At DaySpring, our vision is to see every person experience the life-changing message of God's love. So, as we worked through rough drafts, design changes, edits and details, we prayed for you to deeply experience His unfailing love, indescribable peace, and pure joy. It is our sincere hope that through these Truth-filled pages your heart will be blessed, knowing that God cares about you—your desires and disappointments, your challenges and dreams.

He knows. He cares. He loves you unconditionally.

BLESSINGS!
THE DAYSPRING BOOK TEAM

Additional copies of this book and
other DaySpring titles can be purchased
at fine retailers everywhere.
Order online at <u>dayspring.com</u>
or
by phone at 1-877-751-4347